The Pilgrim among Us

Dear Aunt Janet,
If you look very
carefully, you'll find that
I snuck in a few punches
on your behalf!
Happy holidays
Love, Roberta
November '91

Books by Roberta Spear

Silks, 1980

Taking to Water, 1984

THE
PILGRIM
AMONG US

Roberta Spear

Wesleyan University Press

Published by University Press of New England

Hanover and London

Wesleyan University Press
Published by University Press of New England, Hanover, NH 03755
Printed in the United States of America   5   4   3   2   1
CIP data appear at the end of the book

Some of the poems in this book first appeared in *Field, The Memphis
Review, The Missouri Review, Ploughshares, Raccoon,* and *Redstart;*
"The Uncles," "In the Moon," "Just South," and "The Old Ones at Dawn" in *Poetry.*

I would like to thank The John Simon Guggenheim Foundation and
The Ingram Merrill Foundation for grants which aided in the completion of this book.

for my parents

Moglie e buoi di paesi tuoi.

Contents

Chestnuts for Verdi

Loose, drifting in pools
of black water, the gravel slushes
as a pair of peahens crosses
the path, stabbing for seeds.
The one I gather from a tuft of grass
pushing up the stones
is too large for them: a chestnut,
hard and glazed,
like the belly of a mare
or the unbroken shore of a piano
where a singer leans, pressing out
the notes into the morning's stillness.

And he is there, arched
over the yellowed keys, his silhouette
as soft as the fingers cupped
around this fruit. The sunlight
slips between the salon drapes,
and a wagon filled with
oak, birch, and chestnut
enters the scrolled gate.
Each new stump waits
for the gray lip of soil
with a patience only trees have.
While the birds come and go,
like lovers frightened
by their own strange music.

The paths shoot off everywhere—
into the trees, the fields,
and one to the maestro's door where
a woman waits with her coin dish
to take us in. Into a web of rooms
unlit by the morning, into a silence
as false as the flowers
old women leave on his grave.

Yet the chestnuts bulging
out of her pockets are there
for anyone to see. Now they can
bring fire to a man's touch
and they'll do nicely in a pudding.
And the snow-tipped branches
which they left behind
rise and fall like heavy arms
coaxing the air, keeping
the music of the earth
close to the earth.

Roncole, 1984

4

In Just One Day

The sun is waking in the high, stony cradle
of the Mottarone. It is gathered
into the sycamore's flailing arms,
the pine's sober gaze,
and dipped into black water
until it wails and the water fills
with light and the wailing
is the wind itself, the breath
of St. Julius pushing the small, white boats
across to the other side.

Smack! The woman laughs for God
and all the others as she slaps
the wake with her fat, brown palm,
pretending to kill the dragon and the snakes
that surface in our thoughts
as we near the island.
The boatman chuckles easily,
and her friends wish that they
had thought of flirting,
of kneading the sunlight and wind,
this burly man whose shirt flaps,
like a red flag, on his chest.

She laughs here, but she'll be the first
to kneel down on the cold slate steps
when we reach the shrine,
to kiss the pointed toes of the gold
threaded slippers, to run her fingers
the length of glass, the linen
nipped and tucked
where the curves of a body should be.

And the first to faint when
her eyes meet the empty sockets
of the skull, the grin
of St. Julius returning her passion.

Now that I've taken the water of this lake
into my own hands, I believe
almost anything. That the people
brought their fears here
and watched the last knot snakes
slip away from the mossy banks
to their sad slumber.
That they were chased by a madman
who was once just a man
in a soiled gown, tripping
through the trees and stones.
That the people paid him
with their hearts as the wind
lifted the leaves, spun them,
and let them settle again.
That this man,
who is now a saint, could come
down from his bed of silks,
from his sleep, come down
to this lady laid out cold in ecstasy
and silent for the first time;
that his bones could make
the twin dragons of her breasts
heave and struggle for air . . .

There are things I can't imagine.
Her friends pat her cheeks,
pull her up and make their way
back to the dock. In just one day,
the sun has left the Mottarone
and gone out into the world.
In just one day, it has grown old,
trying to sort the pilgrim
from the rest of us.

Valley Spores

The best ones spring right up
from rain-soaked piles
of dung. My son laughs
as his grandfather tries to explain
how the bruised spring sky
enters an unwilling earth
and works its magic.

On Sunday evenings, I'd stand
at the sink, watching
my father and mother peel back
the pale hides, rinse,
and let them float, stem-up,
until they gleamed, like bowls
set out for creatures even
smaller than I. No chanterelle,
this plain valley spore.
Neither funnel, bell, nor star.
But still, their undersides,
sow-pink at first, would blacken
in the steamy fungal broth.
The silt drifted to the bottom
of our cups as we drank.
And then I kissed them both
and went to bed, half-believing
I might never wake.

The best ones, he goes on,
thrive in the places
you never find, untouched
by ribbons of alkali.

But, if you do, if you climb
the braid of wire at dawn
and leap into the field,
you can see them everywhere,
their bald heads bobbing
in clusters. In stubble,
mud, and witchgrass, hundreds
to fill a bathtub, or
to leave their smeared,
black moons beneath you. Everywhere,
when only seconds before
you looked and nothing bloomed.

Breeding Season

Here, where eucalyptus drag the weir,
cows sink at the water's edge
like soft, milky anchors.
And here, where the Portuguese walked
with their grain pails, watching
for the first slow monarch
to rise in the pasture,
my father pulled into a cloud of dust,
left us waiting one summer evening
while he brought down out of the sky
every wing he could see.

It must have been a mother's instinct,
the sweet twang of mosquito
ascending from the reeds and nettle.
Or the stories you'd hear—
a puff of smoke at the end of the field,
the farmer running, thinking
all the while his crops
were on fire. Or of the one
that nips a child behind the ear,
sucking her life away.
How quickly the glow spread
as my father rubbed the barrel
with an oily rag, preparing
for that season of weapons
useless against the invisible. Whatever,
my mother slammed the truck door hard
and I could hear her heart buzz,

feel her small arms fold around me
as we ran to the nearest house.

o

It's a lucky thing, I think, our bodies
aren't any smaller as they drift
like ribbons of dust into the shade.
For, on those summer nights,
the darkness tapped at our window
and let them enter, fierce,
black orphans clinging
to nothing. As they sprawled,
I clung to my father's ankles,
watching his lips tighten
as he swung them down with a towel,
as the drone diminished
into the night, the black skies
bitten by a single star.

o

Graceless, though they poise
and vibrate, disappear
into cracks. We dream the rain
has washed them down,
their fragile sirens becoming
the music of water held up by stone.

They take our pain with them,
the pain which makes us
hold another, which made me rise
and drift while my son,
in his first month, sucked the moon
and all the burning stars
around it from my breast.

When the fever broke, I wanted
to ask which star had kept us
through those nights when
the small, gray wing in his eyes
fluttered and closed,
and which one brought us back again
to the heat of each day
and to places like this where
the road curves and enters the water,
where my father met his share
of sky and smoke, and smelled
the fragrance of night coming on,
the cows bedded in wet sand,
the nettle, even the wild rose
which he snapped from its brown stem
and took as a gift for my mother and me.

Painting in Fog

The sky won't lift its scowl
from the branches,
so the children crouch beneath them
to paint in the fog.
Their sheets of paper curl
at the edges as the colors run.
They paint doors that open
and close on the mist,
then crawl over the thresholds,
laughing. On days like this,
I could cross a threshold
and never know it.
The woman who lived down the street
thought the fog was her favorite coat
and wandered out in it
barefoot, in a pink slip,
like a frozen lily.
She threw crusts to the children,
hard, black seeds, and moaned
when they wouldn't go away.
Now they think it is her mouth
opening slowly in the branches.

Yet, above them, a space
stretches in all directions.
Through it, you can see another sky,
a dove gliding by with some twigs,

a sprinkling of ash
from a morning fire. It is almost
the curve of a smile,
an arm cradling someone's head
for the last time.
When the boat-shaped leaves
and the black cars line up
at the curb, the children suck
their brushes to fine points.
There are things they haven't yet
learned to paint: the movement
of wheels, the waves of air
through the branches, the warmth
of someone who has passed.
For they have just come here
with their jars of milky water,
their brave slashes of sunlight.

The Uncles

They say that as a young child
you were especially smitten
with older men—those red-nosed,
unmarried uncles of your father.
They held you up until you brushed
the veil of heat that hugged
the ceiling. You could see
the crescent fold of cheek, flesh
pocked and marbled with a hundred
dying rivers. Gold suspenders,
boaters perched atop the thinning,
sweat-soaked domes—touches
of dignity. And the day's first
shot of whiskey smelled like honey
socked inside a willow trunk
where you were queen. You found
a nesting place in their arms
during Sunday drives and funerals.
When the August sun came down square
on the warped anvil of this valley,
you were taken off to nap
in a darkened room at the back
of the house. The elders gathered
on the porch with beer and ham
on buttered bread, or took the path
through sycamores to argue crops
and wars and money. One of them
would slip away to where you rested
in a buttoned slip and socks.

In the angelic haze of late-day
light, he would dip into
the coarse field of his pocket
and lay it there beside you
on the pillow—a coin
as round and silver as the moon
that would rise before you woke.

Sac-ra-men-to, Cal-i-for-nia

The vilest curse
a woman could utter in those days.
Not her husband nor the maid
nor the pigeons on the stoop,
swallowing their portion
of morning light could imagine
such a place. The precise syllables
of a sudden rage: *Sac-ra-men-to,*
whenever her fingers grazed
the rim of a hot skillet
or the iceman left his tracks
in the hall. *Sac-ra-men-to, Cal-i-for-nia,*
if snow came a day early and
without warning. Her accent blackened
the name of that place out west
as though life in this city
were the beginning and end of it.
But, even here in New York,
she had been left behind, this woman
who still double-knotted her apron and
kept fish for the evening's supper
in the bath downstairs. This woman
who powdered her arms with the flour
she had saved for the hens.
A mind both practical and eastern.
But why did her heart keep taking voyages?

Outside, Vyse Avenue
and the first icy winds blow up
wads of news from the grocer's crates.
The new world, she thinks,
first it's seen and then eaten.
Farther down the street,
the sacred wall of the Bronx Zoo
with its huge baskets of parrots,
its sultry leopards. all the creatures
misplaced in this world. Perhaps
she would be the one to lead them
away from the ashen skies
of 1930. Over the stubble
of the plains, over those mythical peaks
to that shadowed city where, they say,
a woman can ripen at night
and flowers open all winter long.
Where dust settles around you,
shimmering, like an oath you take
only once in your life.

Armona

A breeze lifts the orchard dust
and the heavy heart of fruit
lets go. Women and children
line up in the humid corridors
of the packing shed, sharing
the heat, its warped halo.
There is no talk of rest
this day, just the day itself.
And a syrup that makes
the fingers stick together,
like cups set out to gather
more coolness, more darkness,
even after the gifts of summer
are taken back.

Once, on a dare, I walked
five miles at dawn to join them
for the day's orders. If you
could slit a seam and make
the pit leap into the ringing bucket
thirty times in one minute
you had the job.
We worked quickly, rolling
casabas and plums down
the wet, splintered tables,
twisting the stems off
the crotches of fruit. In one,
a small, dark chamber where
a black widow was sleeping,

waiting for the moment
when she and her young could ride
that sweet river into sunlight.
She might have said *pardon me*
or *let me pass in peace,*
but she lunged straight toward me
from her sleep, pleading
like the others for more coolness,
more life. I threw my knife
into a roadside ditch and paced
the miles back to town.
For as sure as the heat had singed
each cloud out of the sky,
that kid who'd dared me here
lay chuckling in his late-morning sleep.

The workers said that once,
years ago, it had happened
much this way. But instead of a boy,
a grown man who called himself
the deacon, who kept two women
and should have known better.
One day, the women came from different farms
to these crumbling sheds
only to discover they'd been peeling
the same peach all along,
dividing its juice. Some said
his shoes were still lashed
to the rafters above us

and, when the wind slid through
the slatted ceiling, they creaked
like the two black doves,
love and death. When we were kids,
we called this town *Aroma*
for the smell of life that has come
and gone, and left its stain
under the nails long after
the black flesh of branches
has dissolved. And for the one
carried down from the rafters,
who wore gloves and a jacket
on the hottest days and loved
the aroma of money, a ripe
freestone, like a piece of ass
with the heart cut out.

How could anyone have known
that the heat would pass?
That, in the shadows, the crisp leaf
of apple, a fork of almond
were springing inch by inch
from the stubble. Or
that a harder season would follow—
One of husks and cores,
and a wind barely getting by,
lifting its soft thumb up
for a ride to another county.

Elegy on Valentine's Day

Like a bundle wrapped
in white cloth, the first light
drops through the old boughs
of camphor. The children kneel
on the ground to open it
and roll it in their sweaters
with their sacks of food and fistfuls
of stones. When I was a child
and you'd ask how much
I loved you, I'd spread my hands,
a small queen setting
the boundaries of sunlight
on the known world.
But your arms were longer
and when it was your turn,
you would take me
a little farther each time.

On the flat edge of town,
the gift of light dissolves
between the rows where a farmer
has set his geese to weed.
And what they don't eat,
he'll cut and scatter, so that
by late afternoon
the whole gray field shimmers
down to the last feather,
the last furred root.

The light makes it clear
who is with us and who has gone.
In my palm, its lacy edges
fill with darkness, with a message
that touches the sky
and pulls the simplest life
from those branches: you are gone.
You have packed your bags
with neither day nor night
but with the dust of this valley
and left it. Then I remember
that when you were young,
this town and its fields were one
and the same and you could say
you came from both
without lying, without having
to hold a stone behind your back.

Now the farmer lifts his hat
to the last train, the caravan
of faces crossing his land
as night overtakes them.
And what did this day have to do
with love? You won't tell me.
And others forget or won't say.
Though the geese whine at its passing.
Though the sky pours itself out
on the cool grass below.

for V. C. S.
1896–1985

26

The Field

There are some creatures who take
all of history with them
when they kneel one last time
in the hard, bitten grass,
only to come back later
with their sense of life,
their nerve as crisp
as a new apple. I called you
Diamond, whom my father
hid like a secret son
in an unmowed pasture. Others
called you *Blackie*, for they
had never seen that wedge
of light under your forelock
or watched you rise at dusk,
lifting up your stallion wings
like huge, gray leaves
into the clouds above them.
Once, years later, your feathered
breath burned through the ice,
bringing a twig, a stone
back to life. Now I take you
for the wind, though my son
crosses the hillside where we walk,
a sprig of juniper in one hand,
the frayed rope of a dream
dangling from the other.

As the day's music begins,
he grasps your mane and pulls
himself onto your pale,
easy curve. How gracefully
you move together through
the throngs of maize and timothy.
The jaws of dust open and close
behind you. And from that
ancient tower staring
down over the fields, crows
fly out to eat the first
high notes tossed up to them,
each seed whipped and broken
by the day, the new light.

In the Moon

1

There are lots of men in the moon,
my son claims, and they all
have dirty feet. Sometimes they march
and the light swells.
Sometimes they lie down
and their mud-caked soles
nearly touch the earth like his
as he races toward the clear
winter sky where earlier
the moon rose between two palms.

2

On a night even colder than this,
she must have been listening
for those soiled boots
moving slowly in her direction.
Anna Akhmatova barely breathed each time
the wind slapped the shutters.
Resting her arms on the crude
wooden table, she pulled
each piece of shell
from the egg she held in her fingers.
''It's like peeling the moon,''
she said. She had brought
this, the first egg of their winter,
to the house of her friends
who watched in silence
as she sliced into thirds
the white, the yolk bruised,

like a sun gone out,
then pushed the plate
in their direction.

3
A single egg all winter—
life being what it was
fifty years before my son's birth.
We must still learn to share
what was never ours.
Whether that rubbery light
which bends to our fancy
or the third translucent slice
of cucumber he sneaks
from the salad. Or the smaller
half-moons of his nails
as he yawns and slips his hand
into mine and we finally
walk side by side,
the dark ring of his lips
making a night all its own.

4
The moonlight is as helpless
as those who tried to gather it
for warmth, like something
you could live by if you had to.
And when those men came down
from there and kicked in

the door to that small room
where the three sat,
kicked over the table and chairs,
the bits of shell scattered,
like a dream, and could
never be found again.

5
In his dreams, he calls out
though he does not wake
or know me. I think
of the crows he heckled today,
the black knives of their wings
cutting the air above us.
Of children's fists thrown up
in play, like stones
at the promise of heaven.
And of that leaf pile
left to darken and crumble,
suddenly let loose so that
the leaves cross the light and,
in falling back to earth,
step toward him.
I think of my own fears
and my love which is greater,
and how I will tell them,
as I tell the others
they must take off their shoes
before they enter.

Conversions

for Ignacio and Norman

At dawn, I hear them
in our yard, my son's two friends
doubled over and cackling, like birds
that fly in from the countryside,
or like two old men crouched
in prayer but for the squeals,
an hysteria that comes and goes
with eight years.

Perhaps, it is the spell of fog
or the scalloped anklets
on that pretty girl who's been warned
to keep her distance.
Most likely though, the faces
their mothers gave them
make them laugh like that—
a sound that echoes
into eternity—and their hard,
black eyes that can measure
a fist or a bottle, a rib
of steam rising from the empty road.

o

Saturdays are different.
In their starched shirts, they climb
the steps to the carved oak doors
of St. John's, and an anthem
of sunlight sweeps down the aisle.

They kneel, cross themselves,
then spring up from the darkened pews
to rush back out into the world.
Only a sparrow nesting in the rafters
arrives first: through a fracture
in the colored glass where Lazarus
has risen, and the wind lets out
a small cry to be filled again
with ashes and scattered blossoms.

o

In this kingdom scarred
by burnt rubber, the names of victims
are sprayed on fences. At night,
the stars spin out like weighted dice.
All our mornings are gray
and stamped with wet leaves.
But while we sleep,
the boys press their faces
into the softened grass
and grip their sides.
As the fog slips from our roof,
their laughter hangs above me.
I wake and go to the window
to scold, to rename them:

St. Ignacio,
St. Norman.

Just South

A cotton gin,
a string of mariachi bars.
So that on a windy day,
the chaff keeps time and insects
do their last dance on the boulevard.
Then, our street with its row
of camphor trees, yellow roses
dusted by first light.
To one side, the twins
hopscotch their tensed, brown arches
neither north nor south,
but in that circle of sisters,
a breeze to keep those
stiff, old branches moving.

Half-asleep, I stand at the sink
adding water, folding
the crumbs of matzo with a wooden spoon.
With one eye on the leeks
propped in a glass,
you wrap your arms around me
and whisper *Happy Pesach*
as though you could free me.
But I am still seeing double—
the girls bending now,
their banners of black hair
sweeping the pavement.

Peso, I think, because I was not
raised among Jews,
but a stone's throw from the vines
and from those who bound them
for little more, those
who saw in the hundreds, the thousands.

And so I go on waking
in this world, hearing double:
the *O*'s of two doves
landing in the branches, hard
and round as the tips
of marimba sticks; of the names,
Moses and *Noah,* and what
was common between us
when he took us in
and one day let us go again
into the sunlight, the wind
making room for everyone.

Graffiti

On a plank fence that faces 6th Street,
the scroll unwinds—
blackened words put down
in the darkness of the night before.
And all we know is what the stars
are willing to tell us
or what the wood beetle mutters
in its borings. The wind strokes
the splintered surface: the hearts and daggers,
bits of swiped oranges, charred
numbers, and the tears of revenge.
This trail should lead back
to the softened corners
where the young doze off
as the sun finally rises. Next door,
our neighbor stands to
tuck in his shirt and goes out
to check the fruit of this day.
With his bucket and brush,
he rants in Armenian, erasing
the message left just for him.
But I try to imagine the rage of Jaime
before it vanishes
and Carlos' courage and who
made Maria feel *that way.* Were you
the one I passed once at dawn
in an empty parking lot,
drawing her gently toward you
and into your leather jacket?

Or the one I saw strutting down
the middle of the street
one freezing night, combing back
your shiny hair with your fingers
as you followed the stars north?
The crows angle downward now,
heckling poor Mr. Bandelian as he
gathers the last, sweet oranges
off the ground. Those birds
drop their black feathers everywhere,
like the scars of old passions
before the earth has a chance
to throw up its arms
and frighten them away.

The Bicycle Thief

My son believes some lazy *cacaroach*
slipped away at dusk
on his small, green bike for a joyride
to the swamps across town.
And I look up for an answer
into the boughs of an elm
where the spokes of sunlight
are spinning wildly. But the truth
rests in the startled eyes
of a woman down the street
who describes *un hombre* tattooed
from here to here,
and her hand sweeps the length
of her body. Then, she points
north to the path he took
when she screamed. Tattooed,
as though the falling leaves
had seared his flesh,
or kisses from lips as dark
as hers had pressed into
his chest, his hips, and ankle bones.

> *Perdido,*
the woman moans, gone forever.
My son stands beside me
on the fiery pavement, barefoot,
his locked knees trying
to forget those endless circles
so recently learned. But then,

he gazes northward up the trail
of lights creeping toward nightfall,
and asks me how far he got as he veered
through the shadows toward home.
His home at the end of the world
where the leaves stew
and black mud pulls on the tips
of branches. Where the earth
wraps its patterned arms
around him and draws him down,
dissolving all traces,
those bright spokes, the wind.

Cita

Here, in our neighborhood,
a woman can be anything
from the scruff of a house slipper
to a breath of smoke warming
the chimney at dawn. She can even
enter the soul of a drunken sparrow
who sings other women to sleep.
But the one who often comes to mind
is Viola, who moved to this city
from Malaga and nightly
sweeps the dirt of others
from her doorway in the alley.
Viola of the tinted skies at dusk,
beating the light out of every
sliver of tin and glass,
whipping up horses of dust that
carry her off to God knows where—
through the alley and farther
than the shaved fields, their manes
smoldering as darkness brings
peace to our labors. Perhaps,
as far as that great ocean
to the west where she can bathe
in the brine of starlight, cleansing
herself of our daily rubbings,
our particles and scraps.

Then they bring her back,
their lathered haunches bearing her
slowly into this valley until
the glint in her eye has become
her own. The men who traffic
the alley at dawn pass by
with a proper respect, their hats
or papers tucked under their arms.
Viola stands once again
in the pale crown of light
that has dropped to her doorstep,
greets them and turns to go in.

Dance

Two trumpets from the Mexican radio station
weave their scales through the dry leaves,
the still morning air.
Across the alley, our neighbor sways
as he hoses off a car so dark,
so weighted down with chrome and leather
that it is sinking inch by inch
into the muddy pool of his yard.
Suddenly, it is easier for me
to stand with my bundle of weeds,
to rise gracefully above the rose and zinnia
broken by a summer wind.
To the waves of music, I would like
to take another by the hand
and go out on a sunlit dance floor,
like a woman I saw once
in a satin skirt whose plump, brown knees
set the direction both she
and her partner would travel.
What keeps one man at a distance
can bring another closer.
Beneath this armful of shattered leaves
and stems that will not budge,
my body shines with sweat. And,
over the fence, I can see
the metal winking back
as he rubs it down with a soft cloth,
a vessel sturdier than these
I'm holding. A safe place
where two could meet in the dark
and find a rhythm to make the stars
and all the life beneath them whisper.

The Old Ones at Dawn

One by one, the scarves of fog lift
off the pier. At last,
you can see them there, their bodies
hunched and dented by the wind.
Back home, their cows have found
the salt mid-pasture; their wives
divide the candled darkness
of first mass. And they have
left their farms, driven
west through the hills
before dawn with their lamps
and oily blankets, to snag a bass
or cod, red-eyed as themselves.

Old and crazy, my father used to say.
Every one of them—Barreiro,
Silva, Rose. Like the names
of those who have slipped from the sea
to sun themselves a few hours
and forgotten to return.
Crazy. And so their wives
have chased them out
to the last, rotted planks
of this half-bridge which will
never take them home.
They drop their lines into
the foam beneath them,
and something calls to them,
these sad, gray angels,
to bend and be silent.

In the roll of a wave,
the deep sigh of Guernsey
ploughed under, the purity
of Charolais. And when
the water lifts and stands
before it funnels,
you can almost see a valley—
not the one they came from
with earth as hard and dry
as the heart wants to make it.

Some Voices

In the last days of October,
when clouds made the shapes of the dead,
we stretched our small bodies out
on the levee and sucked the crimson
out of pomegranate flesh.
Flat on our bellies and trying
to make the willows kiss
the gray water, we watched
their feathery shoots scrawl
on the surface the history of
a leaf flipped over or a stone
punted around the world
and back to this very spot.
A history of anything blessed
both with silence and the power
to break the sluggish surface
into light. Soon, something else
caught my eye: across the river,
the glint of a steel track
tracing the curves of an orchard.
And, peering out at that hour
from the streamer of windows,
faces that made us stand and watch
as though the slope of a cheek
or a waving hand could
bring life to the flatness
of this sky, this land.

o

I always knew where I came from,
but I couldn't believe it.
In childhood dreams, strong tides
carried off the mockingbirds
and the tufts of cotton
exploded in the night,
like Italian stars. At the station
a mile into town, my mother
straightened her stockings
and strangers thrummed on valises
and old uncles bowed, begging
for hugs. The crowd gathered
slowly, all smiles and tears,
until a man in a black cap,
his teeth like a keyboard,
sang out *Leaving for Corcoran.*
And nothing but steam filled the air.

o

Poor Corcoran.
Poor Shafter. Poor Taft.
The blunt steel nose pushes
its way through those
brief exhalations of dust.

Ain't no place to get off,
the man slumped beside me mumbles,

but I'm going there anyway.
A tumbleweed races us through town
and the ricks of cotton
stretch out like bones
along the rails. And he recalls
with a sudden sweetness
old lady Roosevelt back in the '30's
standing on those crates
in a sun hat wide as an ocean liner,
soothing the Okies with words
that swept the dust
right off their bread.

The women still come here, he says—
aunties, daughters, and the rest
to see their folks
at the new prison. Men who'll
leave *after a spell,* remembering
little but the heat and fog,
the sound of wheels grinding
in the middle of nowhere
like a woman's voice
as you fall off to sleep.

o

My son kneels down and places
a penny flat on the rail,

then sifts some gravel
into a pyramid. Seconds later,
he adds the torn sleeve of a foxtail
which has blown his way. Anything
that will let him touch
that huge, steamy body which
he has come to believe
is God. The yellow warning line
still two feet behind him,
he turns his head and rests
his ear on the track,
listening for the distant hum.
But when it comes, he reaches
for my hand and stays close.
The engine grows immense,
hissing; the glint of steel
blinds us. And as we start to
mount the silver steps, I can see
that he has already learned
some voices will take you anywhere.

The Nest

The mockingbird throws open
her wings, and storms off
into the night. Soon
stars fill her empty nest.
The others come to look:
one to snitch a tuft of milkweed,
another to inspect the ragged seams.
Lastly, some stranger
in a black shirt, red cravat,
a mobster by daylight,
claims this hideout for himself
and his honey, the phoebe,
for the sweetness of night
has stunned them both.

Is it possible, all that
spit and polish come to nothing?
Or to those who never knew us,
never felt the ache of mud
and grass, these walls
through which we too will enter,
brushing the last fingers of air?
Already, my daughter
blows bubbles at me, flushes
and stares off at the light
spilling over the edges.

When she leaves, I'll lift
the windows and let them in—
the sparrow will rest on my pillow,
the wind fill my favorite dress.
Even the mockingbird will
pluck the mold and dust
from her feathers, and study
the mirror where I lift my child
to meet herself, and we laugh
at that other nest, shining,
filled with its endless rooms.

Night Song

Each evening, a new rhythm comes
when my foot pumps the rocker
worn down to bare wood.
We sway and doze though the sun
is still licking the sill.
Your eyes flutter open and close
each time the jays screech or
the children in the alley yell.
Why sleep at all, you
so full of this new life? Soon
you'll see how the night gathers up
all those glistening shards,
how it swallows the bickering
of the smallest creature.

Once, long ago, I learned how to
weave the last threads of light
into a ladder for anyone to climb.
For the man I imagined
resting on the roof of our house.
From up there, he could see
the colors rise with the dust
of this valley, and enter
the charred veins of its trees.
My mother didn't believe me.
No one was up there, she said,
or ever would be. But she was wrong.
I had heard the shadows sighing
as the beard of moonlight
swept the ground.

Not a sound now. My children
empty their hands in dreams.
Now I could fly out the window
and join the sparrows
huddled in the trees before dawn.
Or fold a moth back into the darkness
with the pages of this book.
Or I could hold myself
as gently as I've learned
to hold others. And who
would know? Listen:
the creaking branches, the shingles—
the small lights stepping
above us. Listen and sleep.

Geraniums

In the next world, I will be the one
forever pushing open
the warped, green shutters to let
the sunlight enter the room.
The one forever lifting up Sophia
so that she and I can reach out
to stroke the ragged leaves,
the thick, red lips of a geranium.
I recall my father in the last world—
the row of buffed shoes
saluting the flare of ties
at the back of his closet when
he stretched out for the day's
third nap. In his paradise,
the love of his youth
was a Portuguese girl who wove
geraniums into her hair. Once,
in the dark, she held out her arms
and the petals scattered,
like small fires, around them.
No potion could erase the stain
of that flower favored by farmwives,
wrought iron, by Mussolini
and maiden aunts. And who would argue
with a father tightening his fists
in sleep as though clutching
a stem or a slender wrist?
And who would meddle with
a child's vision of heaven when
the brightest in this life
shoots up and spills earthward,
following us into the next?

Dust

1
To survive this season,
you must get used to
the weeping, the crusted ear,
the thickening of the tongue
and brain. My son and I
brave an April wind
filled with its gray ghosts
for a trek to Blanco's bakery
to pick out his birthday cake.
For him, survival is a matter of
blending the grit of dust
with the buttercream stumps
of dinosaurs. He staggers
on the walk beside me, keeping
pace with the wind as it
dances over my shoes
and rises to a full waltz,
wrapping its flighty arms
around me. The pine trees
blanch and shimmer,
the lilies sag on their
last breath. And a pale mask
hides the cheeks of this boy
who blustered into life
six years ago and, like dust,
refused to settle.

2
Just weeks ago, we stood
by my grandmother's grave and
the wind stopped suddenly
as though she wanted to say
one place isn't another,
or to study the dress I had worn
for my visit. Then, the sun
broke through on every blade
and etching, every name
the dust had left behind.
Loam, sand, hardpan, rock—
layer upon layer, until the one
she might have been
and all my names for her
were lost. I laid the flowers down
and called for my child
lounging on a worn stone
to catch the light, the wind.
To feel for a moment
the old warmth of her fingers
stroking his cheek again.

3
A man might imagine an angel
of dust when, with my rags and bristles,
I turn glass back into air,
cheeks into roses.

The first rain and I lock arms, rejoicing.
But if I am *the angel of dust,*
unnamed by the gods
who huddled together, hiding
their eyes in their shawls
through this miserable season,
then what are the sparrows
wheezing in the locust trees?
And the grasshopper who lurches
into the rot of life?
And what are all the stars
reeling in their gritty capes?

4
At the back of the bakery,
in a darkened closet,
an old wooden barrel filled
with granules infinite and white,
as though the cosmos had disrobed
in private for the baker.
He closes the door behind him,
rubs his hands, and smiles
as he moves toward the counter
where we stand. In the light
of day are the dozens
which have risen for him
and will go out into the world
on the sweetened lips of the multitudes.

Row upon row on wire racks—
every color of confection,
powdered and cut, the sudden
rainbows of Creation.
Dust to dust? And I wonder
how we'll survive. Outside,
the sky moves too quickly
and the faces darken
long before night. *Don't worry,*
says Blanco, *a little light,*
a little sugar,
and we take the first bite.

University Press of New England publishes books
under its own imprint and is the publisher for Brandeis
University Press, Brown University Press, Clark University
Press, University of Connecticut, Dartmouth College,
Middlebury College Press, University of New Hampshire,
University of Rhode Island, Tufts University, University of
Vermont, and Wesleyan University Press.

Library of Congress Cataloging-in-Publication Data

Spear, Roberta.
  The pilgrim among us / Roberta Spear.
    p.   cm.
  ISBN 0–8195–2198–1. — ISBN 0–8195–1200–1 (pbk.)
  I. Title.
PS3569.P395P55   1991
811'.54—dc20   91–10658

About the Author Roberta Spear lives in Fresno,
California, with her husband and two children. She grew
up in nearby Hanford, California, and received a B.A. and
M.A. from California State University, Fresno. Her
previous books of poetry are *Taking to Water* (1985), which
won the 1985 Literary Award from PEN, Los Angeles
Center, and *Silks* (1980), published as part of the National
Poetry Prize Series. She has also won the James D. Phelan
Award in Poetry and is the recipient of writing grants from
the NEH, the John Simon Guggenheim Foundation, and
the Ingram Merrill Foundation.

This book was designed by Sally Harris/Summer Hill
Books, Weathersfield, Vermont, and set in Linotron 202
Meridien by Brevis Press, Bethany, Connecticut.